Traditio
Honey

Brigid Barrett

BBNO
The Weaven
Little Dewchurch
Hereford
HR2 6PP

ISBN 0905652 58 4

Contents

FOREWORD

Ireland was once referred to as 'The Land of Milk and Honey' It would still be appropriate to refer to it as such. In a land with plenty of forage for the bees, and the nice damp climate to assist in the secretion of nectar, Ireland produces some of the finest honey in the world.

I hope that you enjoy trying some of these recipes as I have done.

I would like to record my appreciation to Ms Gay Buggy of Foxrock, Dublin 18, who was kind enough to do most of the sketches in this book.

Brigid Barrett
Dublin, 2005

BARBECUE SAUCE 1

1 onion finely chopped
25 g (1 oz) butter.

Method
Fry onion in butter until soft and golden brown. Remove from heat.

Blend in
4 tablespoons of vinegar
2 tablespoons of honey
6 level tablespoons of tomato ketchup
1 tablespoon Worcester sauce
2 level teaspoons of french mustard
4 tablespoons of water
half level teaspoon of salt, pepper.

Stir well and simmer for 30 minutes. Serve with chops, spare ribs, sausages, hamburgers.

BARBECUE SAUCE 2

3 tablespoons tomato ketchup
2 tablespoons brown sauce
$1/3$ cup prepared mustard
1 tablespoon dried mustard
2 tablespoons honey
1 tablespoon freshly ground black pepper
1 tablespoon white vinegar
$1/2$ cup fresh lemon juice
A dash of Tabasco or $1/4$ teaspoon Cayenne pepper
1 tablespoon Worcester sauce
1 tablespoon Soya sauce
2 tablespoons oil
2 teaspoons tomato puree
Minced or crushed garlic

Method
Combine ingredients except the garlic and mix well. Pour into jars and store. May be stored for several weeks in a refrigerator. About two hours before using, add crushed garlic.

CITRUS DRESSING FOR GREEN SALAD

One orange
1 lime
2 tablespoons sunflower oil
1 tablespoon walnut oil
1 tablespoon soy sauce dark
1 tablespoon honey
Salt & pepper

Method
Whisk 2 tablespoons orange juice, lime juice and 1 tablespoon of the grated rind of the orange and lime. Add oils, soy sauce and honey and whisk well. Taste and check the seasoning. To serve place salad leaves in a bowl and pour over the dressing. Toss well and serve immediately.

HONEY-CLOVE GLAZE

$1/2$ cup honey
$1/4$ cup lemon juice
$1/2$ teaspoon ground cloves
2 teaspoons soy sauce

Method
Combine the ingredients in a small screw top jar. Stir to mix well. Heat just before using. Makes $2/3$ cup.

May be used when barbecuing ham or chicken.

LEMON CREAM DRESSING

1 teaspoon lemon juice
2 egg yolks
1 teaspoon honey
1 teaspoon mixed herbs
1 pinch fresh chopped or green dried lemon thyme
1 cup cream or sour cream or yoghurt

Method
Blend the lemon juice with the egg yolks. Stir in honey, herbs and cream. Beat with a wooden spoon until smoothly blended. Use with fruit salad.

(makes half a pint - a delightful accompaniment to any fruit salad)

Fish

HONEYED PLAICE

Serves 4

8 fillets of plaice/lemon sole - skinned
250 g (10 oz) mussel flesh
Juice and rind of 1 orange
1 tablespoon honey
1 tablespoon soy sauce
Freshly milled black pepper

Method
Place mussel flesh on fish fillets. Roll up and arrange in an oven proof dish. Season.
Mix the honey, soy sauce and orange juice together. Pour over the fish.
Bake in a moderate oven 190°C (375°F) Gas 5 for 15-20 minutes.
Serve sprinkled with orange rind.

Calories per serving 205
Suitable for Microwave cooking

By kind permission of An Bord Iascaigh Mhara - The Irish Fisheries Board.

STIR FRY PRAWNS

Serves 4

4 Portions Prawns
400 g (1 lb) cooked brown rice
2 tablespoons of honey
6 tablespoons of white wine vinegar
1 chilli finely chopped - optional
100 g (4 oz) of cooked peas
A little oil

Method
Heat a little oil in a large frying pan or wok. Put prawns and chilli into the pan, cover
and cook for 2 to 3 minutes, stirring occasionally. Add the honey and white wine
vinegar and cook for one minute. Mix the cooked brown rice and peas in with the
prawns and heat through.

Cook's notes:
This recipe uses shelled Dublin Bay prawns (also called langoustine). A portion is between 6 -8 medium sized prawns per person. If you are using frozen prawns make sure you defrost them first.
You can use any vinegar in this recipe, but you may have to adjust the amount of honey, depending on the type of vinegar you use. The easiest thing to do is taste as you go.
If you are using uncooked or frozen peas, add them to the pan at the same time as the prawns and follow the recipe above.

By kind permission of An Bord Iascaigh Mhara - The Irish Fisheries Board.

GLAZED RAY WITH OVEN-ROASTED VEGETABLES

Most people fry ray, but for a more original approach, why not try roasting it with wedges of root vegetables like white turnips, beetroot and baby onions? Marinated briefly in soy sauce with honey and orange juice, the fish is moist and tender and flakes easily off the bone, while the vegetables add their own earthy flavours.

Serves 4

450 g (1 lb) ray
Zest and juice of 1 orange
2 tablespoons honey
4 beetroot - peeled
4 white turnips - peeled
8 small onions
8 cloves garlic
Sprig rosemary
Olive oil
Salt and pepper

Method
Preheat the oven to 200°C (400°F) Gas 6. Make up glaze with orange juice, soy sauce and honey. Pour over ray and marinate for 5 minutes. Brush vegetables with oil, season with salt and pepper. Place on lightly oiled roasting tin. Transfer ray to oven-proof dish and pour over a little of the marinade. Reserve the rest, bring to the boil and reduce to thicken slightly. Put fish and vegetables into oven and roast for 15-20 minutes. Arrange on a serving platter and pour the rest of the sauce over the fish.

You can substitute Rock Salmon or monkfish.

By kind permission of An Bord Iascaigh Mhara - The Irish Fisheries Board.

CHICKEN DRUMSTICKS IN HONEY AND MUSTARD

Preparation time 10 minutes
Cooking time 30 minutes
Oven Temp. 200°C (400°F)

8 chicken drumsticks
25 g (1 oz) butter
2 tablespoons Dijon mustard
2 tablespoons honey
2 tablespoons lemon juice

Garnish: coriander leaves or parsley

Method
Wipe the drumsticks with kitchen paper and cut two or three deep slashes in the flesh
of each drumstick, then place them in a deep bowl. Heat the butter gently in a small
pan until just melted. Mix together the mustard, honey, melted butter and lemon juice
and spread over the.chicken. Leave to marinate for several hours or overnight. Place
the drumsticks on a baking sheet and cover loosely with foil. Bake in a preheated
oven for 20 minutes then remove the foil and baste the chicken with the juices.
Return to the oven for a further 10 minutes or until the juices run clear, when the
drumsticks are pierced with a skewer.

HONEYED LAMB STEW

454 g (1 lb) cubed lamb
1 onion - chopped
1 carrot - sliced
1 small tin chopped tomatoes
1 tablespoon honey
1 pint of chicken stock or 1 stock cube

Method
Season the meat and brown in sunflower oil. Remove and put in casserole. Add onions, carrots and tomatoes and cook for one minute. Add honey and stock. Bring to boil and add to the meat in the casserole. Cover tightly and cook at 190°C (375°F) Gas Mark 5 for 1 to 1 1/2 hours.

CURRY FLAVOURED LAMB CHOPS

4 large lamb chops
4 tablespoons honey
1 tablespoon Soya sauce
1 tablespoon dried mustard
1/4 teaspoon ground ginger
1 rounded teaspoon curry powder
A crushed clove of garlic
Salt and pepper

Method
Preheat the grill to moderate to high. Mix together the honey, Soya sauce, mustard, ginger curry powder, garlic, salt and pepper. Arrange the chops on the grill rack. Paint well with half the honey glaze, and grill for 3 to 5 minutes. Turn the chops over and brush thoroughly with the remaining glaze. Grill for a further 3 to 5 minutes, or until the chops are cooked to your taste. Serve on a bed of creamy mashed potatoes and vegetables of your choice.

LIVER AND ONIONS WITH SWEET AND SOUR SAUCE

450 g (1 lb) lamb's liver very thinly sliced
2 tablespoons vegetable oil
15 g ($^1/_2$ oz) margarine or butter
225-300 g (9-12 oz) button onions
1-2 tablespoons plain flour for coating
salt and freshly ground black pepper
3 tablespoons wine vinegar
6 tablespoons clear honey
freshly chopped parsley to garnish

Method
Heat the oil and margarine in a large frying pan and fry the onions until they begin to soften. Coat the liver slices in flour seasoned well with salt and pepper. Push the onions to one side of the pan and fry the liver slices lightly for about 2 minutes on both sides. Add the wine vinegar and honey to the liver and onions in the pan. Shake the pan and let the mixture bubble for a minute or so. Sprinkle over the fresh chopped parsley. Serve at once, spooning a little of the syrupy sauce over each portion of liver and onions.

HONEY GLAZED PORK CHOPS

4 thick loin pork chops
1 tablespoon vegetable oil
$^1/_2$ pint dry white wine
1 level teaspoon five-spice powder
Juice of 1 orange
2 tablespoons clear honey
Salt and ground black pepper
Garnish - slices of orange

Oven temp: 190°C (375°F)

Method
Heat the oil in a roasting tin. Add the chops and fry over moderate heat until browned on both sides. Pour in the wine, then sprinkle in the five-spice powder and bring to the boil. Remove the tin from the heat and cover with foil, then bake in the preheated oven for 1$^1/_4$ hours until tender. Turn the chops occasionally in the liquid. Remove the chops from the cooking liquid and cut off and discard the fat and rind. Cover the chops with foil and keep warm. Stir the orange juice, honey, and salt and pepper to taste into the juices in the roasting tin. Bring to the boil and simmer stirring all the time until the liquid is reduced to a syrupy glaze – 5 -10 mins. Spoon the glaze over chops, garnish with orange slices and serve immediately.

APRICOT AND HONEY GLAZED PORK RIBS

1 tablespoon honey
1 tablespoon apricot jam
1 teaspoon dried mustard
1 teaspoon Worcester sauce
1 teaspoon of mint sauce

Method
Mix the ingredients and paint on the Ribs during the last 10 minutes cooking.

RED HOT RIBS

Preparation time 8-10 mins
Cooking time $1^1/_2$ hours
Oven temp. 200°C (400°F)

1200 - 1400 g (3-3$^1/_2$ lb) ChInese style pork spare ribs.
2 cloves garlic peeled and crushed
1-2 fresh green chillies, seeded and finely chopped or $^1/_2$ -1 teaspoon chilli powder
to taste
$^1/_2$ in piece fresh root ginger peeled and crushed
3 tablespoons clear honey
3 tablespoons dark soft brown sugar
4 tablespoons tomato ketchup
4 tablespoons dry sherry ~ wine vinegar
2 tablespoons soya sauce
2 tablespoons French mustard
2 tablespoons Hoisin sauce
4 teaspoons chilli sauce or to taste
Salt and ground black pepper
Garnish: spring onion tassels

Method
Put all the ingredients, except the spare ribs and spring onion tassels in a jug and
whisk well until thoroughly mixed. Put the spare ribs in a large roasting tin and pour
over the sauce. Coat the ribs in the sauce until coated all over. Bake uncovered in
the preheated oven for 30 minutes then turn the ribs over and roast for a further 30
minutes. Lower the oven temperature to 180°C (350°F) turn the ribs over again and
continue roasting for a further 30 minutes, or until the sauce is thick and syrupy.
Transfer to a large serving dish and garnish with spring onion tassels.

HAM AND CHEESY ROLLS

8 cheese slices
8 slices of cooked ham
150 g (6 oz) cottage cheese
Freshly ground black pepper

The Sauce:
15 g ($^1/_2$ oz) butter
1 tablespoon oil
1 small onion finely chopped
1 clove of garlic - crushed
400 g (1 lb) can chopped tomatoes
1 dessertspoon honey
1 teaspoon mixed herbs or basil
Salt and freshly ground black pepper

Method
Melt the butter with the oil in a saucepan and lightly cook the onion and garlic until soft. Add the rest of the ingredients. Bring to the boil. Lower the heat, cover and simmer for 30 minutes. Add seasoning to taste. Place a slice of cheese on each slice of ham. Season the cottage cheese with pepper and herbs, and divide evenly between the ham and cheese slices. Roll up and place in a single layer in an oven-proof dish with the joins underneath. Pour the tomato sauce over the ham slices, and cook in the oven for 10 minutes, until bubbling. A mixture of grated cheese and breadcrumbs may be tossed over the top before baking.

SPICY HONEY GLAZED HAM

$^1/_2$ ham ready cooked
2 tablespoons honey
1 teaspoon ground ginger
1 teaspoon horseradish sauce

Method
Remove skin from the ham when slightly cooled. Mix together the honey, ginger and horseradish and spread over the ham. Return to the oven and bake until golden – about 20 minutes.

POTATOES WITH HONEY AND MUSTARD

5 new potatoes
A tablespoon of chopped fresh mint

Mustard dressing:
3 tablespoons yoghurt
1 dessertspoon grain mustard
1 teaspoon Dijon mustard
1 teaspoon honey
1 tablespoon olive oil
Salt and freshly ground black pepper

Method
Cook scrubbed potatoes in boiling salted water with a hint of mint until cooked.

Make the dressing as follows:-to the yoghurt add the mustards honey and olive oil in a small saucepan. Season to taste with salt and pepper. Heat gently, stirring. Do not boil. Drain the potatoes and pour the heated sauce over the potatoes. Garnish with chopped mint. Serve at once.

CHOCOLATE AND TOFFEE SHORTBREAD

Makes 20 squares

For the shortbread:
100 g (4 oz) margarine or butter
50 g (2 oz) caster sugar
50 g (2 oz) corn flour
100 g (4 oz) plain flour

For the topping:
175 g (6 oz) plain chocolate

For the filling:
100 g (4 oz) margarine or butter
100 g (4 oz) soft light brown sugar
30 ml/2 level tablespoons honey
60 ml condensed milk
$1/4$ teaspoon vanilla essence

You will require
Swiss roll tin lightly greased
Set oven to moderate 180°C (350°F) Gas 4.

Method
SHORTBREAD -Place margarine/butter and sugar in a bowl, cream together until light and fluffy. Sift corn flour and plain flour together, then gradually beat into the creamed mixture. An electric mixer does this process quickly and smoothly. Knead lightly, then press mixture into the prepared tin, using the back of a wooden spoon. Bake for 25 minutes in the centre of the oven. Leave to cool.

FILLING - Place the filling ingredients in a saucepan and melt over a low heat until the margarine/butter and sugar have melted. Bring to the boil and cook for 7 minutes, stirring constantly. Pour over the shortbread and leave to set.

TOPPING - Melt the chocolate for the topping in a bowl over a pan of hot water. Pour over the filling, and leave to set, then cut into 20 squares

AFTERNOON TEA CAKES

150 g (6 oz) self raising flour
100 g (4 oz) margarine or butter
75 g (3 oz) sugar
2 eggs
Teaspoon honey
Grated rind of lemon
Half teaspoon vanilla essence

Preheat oven at Gas mark 5

Method
Cream margarine, sugar and honey. Gradually add the beaten eggs and vanilla essence. Fold in flour and lemon rind. Spoon into two patty tins. Bake one above the other for about 10 minutes interchanging the tins after 8 minutes. Makes approximately 18 cakes.

FLAPJACKS

100 g (4 oz) butter
25 g (1 oz) sugar
2 tablespoons honey
200 g (8 oz) Irish oatflakes
$1/2$ teaspoon salt
1 level teaspoon of ground ginger or cinnamon - optional.

Method
Cream the butter and sugar. Stir in the honey, add in the oats salt and spices (if used) Put mixture into a well greased shallow tin with straight sides and press into position with a knife or spatula. Bake in a moderately hot oven 190°C (375°F) Gas 5 for 30-40 minutes.

Cut into rectangular shapes and leave in the tin until cold.

GINGERBREAD MEN

250 g (10 oz) self raising flour
Pinch salt
50 g (2 oz) margarine
100 g (4 oz) caster sugar
3 teaspoons ground ginger
3 tablespoons honey
Currants or sultanas
Glacé cherries

Method
Grease 2 baking trays. Sieve flour, salt and ginger. Heat margarine, honey and sugar until melted. Stir into the dry ingredients and mix well. Leave until firm and cool enough to handle. Shape into small figures and place on to the baking trays. Mark eyes with currants or sultanas and put a few currants down the 'body'. Use a small piece of cherry for the mouth. Bake on the middle shelf at 170°C (335°F) Mark 3. Ease from tray with a palette knife and leave on a wire tray to cool.

HAZELNUT AND HONEY CHEESECAKE

150 g (6 oz) digestive biscuit crumbs
75 g (3 oz) butter or margarine
100 g (4 oz) hazelnuts
200 g (8 oz) cream cheese
4 tbsp clear honey
2 eggs, separated
$1/2$ oz powdered gelatine
2 tbsp water
8 fl oz double cream

Method
Mix together the biscuit crumbs and butter and press into the base of a 9 inch loose-bottomed flan tin. Reserve a few hazelnuts for decoration and grind the remainder. Mix with the cream cheese, honey and egg yolks and beat well. Meanwhile, sprinkle the gelatine on the water leave to stand until spongy. Place the bowl in a pan of hot water and stir until melted. Stir into the cheese mixture with the cream. Whisk the egg whites until stiff, and gently fold them into the mixture. Spoon over the base and chill until set. Garnish with the whole hazelnuts.

HEALTHY BISCUITS

75 g (3 oz) plain flour
75 g (3 oz) wheaten flour
125 g (5 oz) flake meal
100 g (4 oz) caster sugar
1 teaspoon bread soda
3 teaspoons ground ginger
125 g (5 oz) margarine
2 tablespoons milk
$1^1/2$ tablespoons honey

Method

Melt margarine, milk and honey together in a saucepan. Add other ingredients and mix well. Form into a sausage shape 1¹/₂ inches in diameter. Slice vertically and place the slices on a greased baking tray. Bake for 20 minutes approx - Gas Mark 3.

HONEY AND ALMOND CAKE

225 g (9 oz) carrots grated
65 g (2¹/₂ oz) almonds finely chopped
2 eggs
100 g (4 oz) or ¹/₃ cup clear honey
4 tbsp oil
¹/₄ pt milk
100 g (4 oz) wholemeal flour
25 g (1 oz) plain flour
2 tsp ground cinnamon
¹/₂ tsp baking soda (bicarbonate of soda)
A pinch of salt
Lemon glacé icing
A few flaked almonds to decorate

Method

Mix together the carrots and nuts. Beat the eggs in a separate bowl, then mix in the honey, oil and milk. Stir into the carrots and nuts, then fold in the dry ingredients. Spoon into a greased and lined 20cm/8 in cake tin and bake in a preheated oven at 150°C (300°F) for 1-1¹/₄ hours until well risen and springy to the touch. Leave to cool in the tin before turning out. Drizzle with the lemon glacé icing, then decorate with flaked almonds.

HONEY AND BUTTERMILK BISCUITS

50 g (2 oz) butter or margarine
200 g (8 oz) self raising flour
6 fl oz buttermilk
3 tbsp clear honey

Method

Rub the butter or margarine into the flour until the mixture resembles breadcrumbs. Stir in the buttermilk and honey and mix to a stiff dough. Place on a lightly floured surface and knead until smooth, then rollout to ³/₄ inch thick and cut into 2 inch rounds with a biscuit cutter and bake in a preheated oven at 230°C (450°F) for 10 minutes until golden brown.

HONEYED APPLE TART

75 g (3 oz) butter or margarine
150 g (6 oz) wholemeal flour
A pinch of salt
1 tsp clear honey
1 egg yolk
$1/2$ tbsp cold water

For the filling:
800 g (2 lb) cooking apples
2 tbsp water
5 tbsp clear honey
Grated rind and juice of 1 lemon
25 g (1 oz) butter or margarine
$1/2$ teaspoon ground cinnamon
2 eating apples

Method
To make the pastry, rub the butter or margarine into the flour and salt until the mixture resembles breadcrumbs. Stir in the honey. Beat the egg yolk with a little of the water and stir into the mixture, adding enough additional water to make a soft dough. Wrap in clingfilm and chill for 30 minutes.

To make the filling, peel, core and slice the cooking apples and simmer gently with water until soft. Add 3 tbsp of the honey, the lemon rind, butter or margarine and cinnamon and cook uncovered until reduced to a puree. Allow to cool. Roll out the pastry on a lightly floured surface and use to line a 8 inch flan ring. Prick all over with a fork, cover with greseproof paper and fill with baking beans. Bake in a pre-heated oven at 200°C (400°F) Gas 6 for 10 minutes. Remove the paper and beans. Reduce the oven temperature to 190°C (375°F) Gas 5. Spoon the apple puree into the case. Core the eating apples without peeling them then slice them thinly. Arrange in neatly overlapping circles on top of the puree. Bake in the pre-heated oven for 30 minutes until the apples are cooked and lightly browned.

Place the remaining honey in a pan with the lemon juice and heat gently until the honey dissolves. Spoon over the cooked flan to glaze.

HONEY BREAD

50 g (2 oz) butter
25 g (1 oz) sugar
$1/4$ tsp salt
$3/4$ tsp mixed spice
1 egg
2 tbsps honey
200 g (8 oz) self raising flour
2 tbsps milk

Method
Cream butter and sugar. Beat in honey. Add dry ingredients to creamed mixture with the whisked egg and milk. Put in a well greased tin and bake in a moderate oven for 40 to 45 minutes.

HONEYBEE BISCUITS

100 g (4 oz) butter
100 g (4 oz) plain flour
2 level tablespoons honey
Chopped glacé cherries
$1/4$ teaspoon of vanilla essence

Method
Cream butter and honey until light and fluffy, add vanilla essence and mix well. Add sieved flour gradually. Flour hands and roll small amounts of the mixture into balls of three sizes. Place three balls together, one under the other on a greased baking sheet to form one biscuit (make it look like a honeybee!). Flatten slightly and sprinkle with chopped cherries. Bake in a moderately hot oven 190°C (375°F) gas mark 5 for 10 to 15 minutes. Cool on a wire tray.

HONEY CAKE

100 g (4 oz) butter
75 g (3 oz) icing sugar
2 tablespoons clear honey
1 level teaspoon chocolate powder
1 tablespoon sherry
200 g (8 oz) crushed Rich Tea/Marietta biscuits

To decorate
$1/4$ pint cream
grated chocolate or chopped cherries

Method
Cream butter, gradually beat in icing sugar and honey until light and fluffy. Beat in grated chocolate and sherry. Stir in crushed biscuits. Turn the mixture into a well greases 7 inch or 8 inch flan ring on oiled greaseproof paper. Chill for two hours. Remove from tin. Whip cream stiffly. Spread over top of cake and decorate with grated chocolate.

LEMON AND CASHEW CRUNCHIES

1 cup flour
$1/4$ tsp salt
1 cup cashews, finely chopped
$3/4$ cup sugar
$1/2$ cup honey
8 tblsp butter
1 tsp lemon juice
Zest of 2 lemons finely grated
1 tblsp lemon juice

Method
Preheat oven to 175°C (350°F). Butter or oil a heavy baking sheet. Combine flour, salt and cashews in a large bowl. Combine the brown sugar, honey and butter in a heavy sauce pan and bring to a boil. Add to the flour with the lemon zest and juice and mix well. Drop batter in $1/4$ teaspoon balls 2 inches apart and bake until the edges are light brown, for 9 to 10 minutes. Cool slightly before removing from baking sheet. Makes 6 dozen.
Other nuts of your choice may be used instead of the cashew nuts.

EASY APPLE MOUSSE

2 egg whites
2 cups chilled apple puree
2-3 tablespoons honey
Grated rind of half a lemon
2 dessertspoons of whiskey or brandy, optional.

Method
Whip egg whites until stiff. Combine with apple puree, honey, lemon rind and brandy folding carefully. Spoon into serving dishes and garnish with grated chocolate, serve cold.

HONEY ICE

One pint cream
Three quarters cupful honey
One cupful milk
One teaspoon flavouring essence

Method
Warm milk, add honey and stir until melted. Mix with the cream, flavour and freeze.

HONEY MOUSSE

50 g (2 oz) honey
4 eggs separated

Method
If the honey is set place the jar in a bath of warm water to liquify it. Mix the egg yolks with the liquid honey. Cook over a very low heat or in a double boiler until the mixture thickens like custard. Whisk the egg whites until stiff and fold them into the honey mixture. Pour into serving dishes and chill for several hours.

ICE CREAM SUNDAE

Pour honey over ice cream, sprinkle nuts on top and garnish with a cherry This is a delicious and nutritious dessert.

LEMON FLUMMERY

2 lemons
1 pint of water
38 - 50 g (1^1/$_2$ oz -2 oz). cornflour
2 eggs
75 g (3 oz) sugar
2 tablespoons honey (or to taste)

Method
Wash and dry lemons. Peel off rind thinly (like potatoes) Put rinds into saucepan, add wate and bring to boil. Blend cornflour with juice of lemons. Strain hot liquid onto it, stirring well. Return to saucepan and cook for about 7 minutes. Cream yolks of eggs with sugar and honey, and pour the hot lemon mixture on to them. Put back on heat for a few minutes to cook the eggs – do not allow to boil. Allow to cool for a few minutes. Beat white of eggs stiffly and fold into lemon mixture. Pour into wet mould or individual dishes to set. Decorate with cherries and cream if liked.

NUTTY RAISIN TREATS

Half cup chopped mixed nuts
^{3}/$_4$ cup low fat milk
50 g (2 oz) raisins or sultanas
Half a cup honey
Half a cup of Rice Krispies

Method
Put all ingredients into a bowl and mix well with spoon. Chill for one hour and serve. Makes about twenty treats.

POACHED PEACHES/NECTARINES WITH BASIL

6 peaches (can be under ripe)
Juice of two oranges
$1/4$ pint of water
25 g (1 oz) caster sugar
2 dessert spoons honey
3-4 leaves of fresh basil.

Method
Put juice and water in a saucepan with the sugar. Stir gently until sugar is dissolved. Add the cut peaches with their skins on (this gives a lovely colour to the syrup). Poach gently until tender. Finely chop 3-4 basil leaves and add to the syrup. Serve hot or cold.

Index of Recipes

Notes

Notes